A Spider, Some Thread, and a Labyrinth Walk:

Sacred Journeys of the Heart Stories
Plus Useful Information about Labyrinths

by Connie Dunn

"Your life is a sacred journey. And it is about change, growth, discovery, movement, transformation; continuously expanding your vision of what is possible, stretching your soul, learning to see clearly and deeply, listening to your intuition, taking courageous challenges at every step along the way. You are on the path... exactly where you are meant to be right now... And from here, you can only go forward, shaping your life story into a magnificent tale of triumph, of healing of courage, of beauty, of wisdom, of power, of dignity, and of love."

- Caroline Adams

NOTE:

The Labyrinth is often used to represent our life's sacred journey. Walking a Labyrinth can be similar to life quests or pilgrimages.

for Judy Swaim and all her work with labyrinths

for the labyrinth committee at First Universalist Society in Franklin (MA)

for my daughter, Michelle, who edits all my work

for my daughter, Erin, who has walked labyrinths with me
and helped build them with me

for my wonderful and supportive wife, Joyce,
who also walks labyrinths with me

for all lovers of labyrinths!

A Spider, Some Thread, and a Labyrinth Walk

A Spider, Some Thread, and a Labyrinth Walk © 2011 Connie Dunn

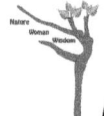

Published by Nature Woman Wisdom

First Edition. Printed and bound in the United States of America.

All rights reserved. No part of this book may be reproduced in any form or by any electronic or mechanical means, including information storage and retrieval systems, recording, or photocopying, without permission in writing from the publisher, except by a reviewer, who may quote brief passages in review or where permitted by law.

Copyright © 2011 Connie Dunn
ISBN-13: 978-0615582658 (Nature Woman Wisdom)
ISBN-10: 0615582656

Published by Nature Woman Wisdom

Printed in The United States of America

December, 2011
 10 9 8 7 6 5 4 3 2

Library of Congress Cataloging in Publication Data

Dunn, Connie

    A Spider, Some Thread, and a Labyrinth Walk

Labyrinth

    A Spider, Some Thread, and a Labyrinth Walk
    by Connie Dunn

Meditation

    A Spider, Some Thread, and a Labyrinth Walk
    by Connie Dunn

Peace

    A Spider, Some Thread, and a Labyrinth Walk
    by Connie Dunn

Stories

    A Spider, Some Thread, and a Labyrinth Walk
    by Connie Dunn

TABLE OF CONTENTS

A Spider, Some Thread, and a Labyrinth Walk 7
The Children's Monastery 13
Grandmother Spider 15
The Peace Quilt 17
Spin, Spin, Spin, and the Thread Flows! 19
Silence Is More than Just Not Speaking 23
Ariadne's Thread 25
Sophia's Many Colored Coat 29
Bramble of Pincup Springs 35
Peace Begins with Me 39
The Star Keeper 43
Mrs. Korovski's Magical Butterfly Garden 45
Eileen of Skellig Bog 47
About the Labyrinth 53
    How to Use a Labyrinth? 54
    Chakras and the Labyrinth 55
    Dancing the Labyrinth 56
    The Labyrinth and Its Meaning 57
    The Labyrinth and the Hopi Symbol 58
    Creating a Labyrinth 59
    The Pilgrimage 64
    Meditation 67
    Journeying and Directed Dreaming 68
    Images in Journeying and Directed Dreaming .. 70
    Mandalas 71
About Magic 75
    Meanings of Magic 76
    Real Magic and Where You Find It 77
    The Magic of Imagination and Storytelling 78
About the Author 79

A SPIDER, SOME THREAD, AND A LABYRINTH WALK

Have you ever experienced an odd combination of events that put together make a rather profound revelation? Well, that's exactly what happened to Grace Witherspoon!

At her church, there is a labyrinth tucked away in a grove of trees. If you weren't as curious as Grace, you might never know it was there. Grace had attended the same church since she was born, and at eight years old, she figured that she knew just about everything anyone needed to know about her church.

One day, Grace's mom was in a meeting and it was a gorgeous fall day, so Grace asked if she could play outside. Her mom gave her the perimeters where she could play safely. Grace might have rolled her eyes at Mom giving her boundaries, but she was very excited to get outside to play. Grace went to find her borders; one was the grove of trees.

"Grove of trees?" Grace asked of no one. "Hmmm. Is that the grove of trees?"

Grace went to check it out. It was a bunch of trees with sort of a hole in the middle. She wasn't sure, but she thought that's what Mom meant by a grove of trees.

"Wow!" she yelled. "There's a labyrinth in there! I've never been in here before!"

Grace went into the grove and began examining the labyrinth. She had only seen a labyrinth one other time and it was a small labyrinth that you walked with your finger. Grace remembered that walking the labyrinth was a sacred activity.

She walked around the outside of the labyrinth until she saw a huge spider web with a beautiful, large, yellow and black, garden spider. "Hello, Ms. Spider," said Grace. "You've been a very busy girl!" Grace found a place to sit where she could watch the spider.

When her mom was finished with her meeting, she went hunting for Grace and found her sitting mesmerized by the spider. Mom smiled. Then, she went over and let Grace know she was there.

"Hi, Mom, isn't she beautiful?"

"Yes."

"Would it be bad if I wanted her for a pet?"

"Not bad, Grace, but a little impractical. You see what beauty she creates? If you were to take her, then what would happen to her web? Where would she be able to spin such shimmery threads?"

"Her web would stay where it is," said Grace with much authority. "She could spin another web."

"Not one as large as this."

"Okay, I'll leave her, but we have to come check on her every day, okay?"

"Deal!" said Mom.

"Deal!" said Grace.

"Want to walk the labyrinth," asked Mom.

"Yes," said Grace.

Mom walked around the labyrinth to the entrance and Grace followed. Mom put her hands together in a prayerful manner, then bowed from the waist while she kept her eyes focused on the center of the labyrinth. After Mom started walking, Grace stepped up to the entrance and did the same things Mom had done.

After they had finished walking the labyrinth, Mom asked? "Have I ever told you the story of the labyrinth?"

"No," said Grace.

Mom told her the story of Ariadne's Thread:

> *There was on the island of Crete (Creet) a king named King Minos (Mine-us). He was married to Pasiphae (Pass-ih-fae), who was the daughter of the sun-god Helios (Hee-lee-us). King Minos and Pasiphae had a daughter named Ariadne (Are-ree-ahd-nee).*
>
> *However, also on this island of Crete, there was a monstrous creature named Minotaur (Mine-oh-tar). Pasiphae did not want the monster killed, so instead Daedalus (Die-dah-lus), an architect and inventor from Athens, built a prison for the creature. The prison was a labyrinth but with large rooms.*

The Minotaur only ate human flesh, so imprisoning the monster was necessary to protect Crete. However, when the monster required to be fed, it bellowed loudly—so loud, that the entire palace shook. Therefore, the king had to feed the monster to keep him quiet.

King Minos had to go to war to keep the monster fed. He fed all the prisoners of war to the Minotaur. On another occasion, one of King Minos' sons visited Athens and was accidentally killed. King Minos was furious and demanded that Athens supply seven maidens and seven male youths every nine years. These young people were to be sacrificed to the Minotaur. By supplying the youth, King Minos promised that Crete would not destroy Athens.

King Aegeus (Age-ee-us) , the king of Athens, also had a son named Theseus (Thes-e-us), who had gained a reputation of slaughtering all the monsters that crossed his path. He took the place of one of the youths going to Crete so he could kill the monstrous Minotaur who had taken the lives of so many of the Athenian youth. He told his father that he would sail with black sails and return with white sails to signal his success.

When Ariadne saw Theseus, she fell in love. As was the tradition, when the young people from Athens arrived, they were all locked into the dungeon. Theseus was to be the first of his youth to go to the Minotaur's prison, but Ariadne did not want him to die. She went to Daedalus and begged him to help her save Theseus.

Daedalus, being a good man at heart and an Athenian who may have known that Theseus was the king's son, agreed to help. He gave Ariadne a magic ball of thread. She was instructed to take Theseus to the gate of the labyrinth, tie one end of the threat to the gate so he could find his way back and give him the ball. He was to roll the ball of thread ahead of him. Once he found the Minotaur and did his deed, then he could follow the thread back out.

Ariadne went to Theseus and made him promise to marry her and carry her away with him if she helped him. Theseus gladly agreed and Ariadne gave him her ball of thread.

> Theseus killed the Minotaur and followed Ariadne's thread back to the entrance. With Ariadne, Theseus freed the Athenian youth and set sail for Athens.
>
> While this love story is lovely, Ariadne was not to marry Theseus. Dionysus, one of the Olympian gods, wanted Ariadne for his own bride. Therefore, Dionysus made a bargain with Theseus for Ariadne. She was sad and wept at the loss of Theseus, but soon married Dionysus and had many sons that became kings of the surrounding islands.
>
> Daedalus, however, was in big trouble with King Minos. Not only did Theseus kill the Minotaur and free the Athenian prisoners, he took his lovely daughter, Ariadne. King Minos learned quickly that Daedalus had helped Ariadne. The king placed both Daedalus and his son, Icarus, in prison. Daedalus later built two sets of wings and the two escaped their prison only to plunge to their death in the sea after getting too close to the sun, which melted the wax that held the wings together.
>
> While many have wondered about the Minotaur's prison, the design of the labyrinth is knows as Ariadne's Thread or the seed pattern. Labyrinths have one way in and one way out. It is thought that the labyrinth because of its many rooms and passageways caused the Cretans and Athenians to become disoriented and lost. Fear also had a factor, because when the Minotaur was hungry, he bellowed very loudly.

"Mom," said Grace, "The thread that Ariadne gave to Theseus…well, it just reminded me of the big spider web that the big garden spider wove over there." Grace pointed in the direction of the beautiful web she had been studying when Mom came to find her.

"Yes," said Mom, "It does all fit together. Remember the story of Grandmother Spider and how she drew the lines that crossed each other to make the four seasons?"

"Like a plus sign?" asked Grace.

"Yes," said Mom, "Just like a plus sign. Can you see that in the middle of the labyrinth?"

Mom walked over to the center of the labyrinth and pointed out the "plus sign."

"Wow!" said Grace. "So all you need is a spider, some thread, and a labyrinth walk!"

Mom smiled and shook her head, "Yes."

"And," Grace said, "we also need two stories!"

They both laughed

A Spider, Some Thread, and a Labyrinth Walk

THE CHILDREN'S MONASTERY

Rev. Silby, the religious education minister at Green Springs Church, told the children during children's chapel about visiting a monastery on his sabbatical, which is sort of like a vacation for ministers only instead of vacationing they do research or study. He told them that the monks, the men who lived in the monastery, had taken a vow of silence.

All the children were amazed. They asked him if he talked at all. Of course, he didn't, because you had to take the same vow of silence to stay at the monastery. They were also curious about how long he stayed, what happened if he hurt himself, what did he do if he needed help from someone, and about a million other questions?

Rev. Silby answered, "I didn't use my voice, at all. I could communicate in other ways...but only when necessary."

When the children's chapel service was nearly over, Rev. Silby asked the children to do something very different. He asked them to be silent for one full minute.

Jonathan thought he might burst. Alyn suppressed a giggle. Mary got the hiccups. Ben knocked over a trash can that made a very loud noise. Zoe left the room so she could burst out laughing.

When the chapel service was over, Logan asked, "Is there a Children's Monastery?"

Rev. Silby said, "Not that I know of, but what a good idea that would be!"

Later that day, the children decided to create a Children's Monastery. Jonathan said, "I think there'd be a labyrinth. My mom likes to walk the one in Oak Cliff."

Mary added that her mom liked yoga. And Alyn said, "I bet there'd be some sort of meditation...but it would be quiet...maybe like sitting still on a bench looking at the garden or something."

They wrote all their ideas down and took them to Rev. Silby, who suggested that they create a Children's Monastery the very next Sunday during their religious education time.

Rev. Silby sent out letters to all the children in the church to tell them what to expect. He even created a giggling pole and put it way out in the playground. He said, "That way if you just have to giggle, you have a place to do it."

The very next Sunday, Rev. Silby had put up signs saying, "QUIET PLEASE! YOU ARE ENTERING THE CHILDREN'S MONASTERY."

Mary and Alyn noticed the big labyrinth drawn on their chapel floor. A labyrinth is sort of like a maze only there is no way to get lost. There is one way in and one way out. The girls began to walk the labyrinth. Although the pattern on the floor didn't look that big, it took awhile to walk it.

Jonathan came and joined the girls in walking the labyrinth. He was very intentional in his walking. He first bowed to the labyrinth, as if he were thanking the labyrinth for allowing him to walk it. Then he walked very slowly and precisely within the walls of the labyrinth pattern. It looked like he was dancing in slow motion. When he got to the center, he again bowed. He walked back out in the same slow dance.

Alyn found the yoga cards spread out in another area that Rev. Silby had prepared for them. She found a mat and began to make the shapes. But she began to get the giggles. At first, she controlled them, but finally she decided she could not. She went out to the giggle pole. There were others at the giggle pole. They were all laughing and talking. But Alyn didn't want to talk and she didn't want to laugh or giggle either. So, before she got there, she went back inside and finished her yoga.

Then she explored the rest of their area for other silent activities. She put on the headphones and listened to music and a guided meditation. She sat in the garden quietly. She walked the labyrinth again.

Rev. Silby rang a chime when Children's Chapel time was over. Before Alyn left, she whispered to Rev. Silby, "I learned a lot today by being silent. I feel more peaceful inside."

Rev. Silby smiled at her and at having a successful Children's Monastery, even if it was just for a day.

GRANDMOTHER SPIDER
(RETOLD NATIVE AMERICAN MYTH)

Before the world existed, there was Grandmother Spider. She thought about the world; and it was. Thinking in this way, she created the world. Then she drew lines that crossed each other. These were the directions and the powers of Native American Spirits. These were the seasons. In all four directions, Grandmother Spider sang. And in the center where the lines crossed, she placed two small medicine bundles.

Grandmother Spider sat in the center of the Universe and sang. And she sang in midst of the waters. In the heavens, she sat on the clouds as she sang. And she sang as she created all the worlds...of the spirits, of the people, of the creatures, and of the gods. And she placed her song upon the face of heaven. And upon the face of the water, she placed her song. And she separated all that she created as she placed her song upon them. Grandmother Spider then placed her will upon the separate seasons. And weaving her design, she sang and thought. Within each of the sacred pouches, Grandmother Spider had placed the seeds that would bear two women: Uretsete and Naotsete. From their baskets would come all that lives. She placed one in the northwest and the other in the northeast.

And as she sang, the pouches swelled. And as she danced, the seeds became women. And that is one reason that the women of our people--the Native American people--have always given reverence to seeds and saved them and honored them. Seeds are eaten. As we eat the seeds, they remind us of our generation. We keep these seeds in sacred places, such as our altar or place of power.

Now, as Grandmother Spider sang and danced, the sisters awoke. They would give human form to the spirit which was the people. Singing, they awoke in the darkness that is below--or in the firmament--that is the place of the Spider. Singing as they awoke, they sat near the Grandmother Spider, who sang as she wove her silken thread.

Grandmother Spider thought long and sang. She knew that one was She Who Matters and the other was She Who Remembers, so they were named Uretsete and Naotsete. And the women made their lives on the Earth, which Spider woman had made from her thoughts as she sang and spun and wove the beautiful threads.

As the two women sat with Grandmother Spider, they took up their work--the work of the sisters who would populate the world.

The sisters said, "We will name. We will think." And that is what they did. They sang. And they chanted in the way of the people. And they made all the languages and tongues of the Earth. They finished everything beautifully. And they named all they had created.

Shaking, Uretsete named the sun and the stars. Shaking, Naotsete thought about the sun and the stars. Singing, they made the sun and the stars. And in the same manner, they sang making the elements: the rains, the thunders, the winds and the snows. Shaping the spirits, the two made the mountains, the valleys, the rivers, the lakes, the animals, the birds, the fish, and the other creatures of the earth. Singing, chanting, crooning, they named each, making ready the earth for their children.

And Uretsete divided the waters and the land, saying the water and the land have become good. Naosete said only the Earth will be ripe. Upon the Earth, our people will live.

The two sisters sent their thoughts into the void. They sang and chanted and thought of their Grandmother Spider. And knew that all was finished and everything was in place for the people.

THE PEACE QUILT

Brianna and Mackenzie ran down the stairs, because that's how they always went down the stairs to Church School on Sunday mornings. They were always eager to be in class or play games or do just about anything…together!

Today was a special day. It was *World Peace Sunday*. Brianna and Mackenzie weren't absolutely sure what that meant, but they were excited about it anyway. Brianna got to lead the *Ghandi Peace Greeting*:

> *I offer you peace.*
> *I offer you friendship.*
> *I offer you love.*
>
> *I see your beauty.*
> *I hear your needs.*
> *I feel your feelings.*
>
> *My wisdom comes from a higher source.*
> *I honor that source in you.*
> *Let us work together.*

Mackenzie led the *Navaho Peace Prayer*:

> *Before me is peaceful.*
> *Behind me is peaceful.*
> *Under me is peaceful.*
> *Over me is peaceful.*
> *Around me is peaceful.*

A Spider, Some Thread, and a Labyrinth Walk

Brianna and Mackenzie discovered that the idea of peace wasn't new. Every Sunday, the Ghandi Peace Greeting was recited by their class. Today, they were asked to think about a time when they quarreled. Both Brianna and Mackenzie could identify with that, because they both had older sisters with whom they quarreled often.

But what did fighting with their siblings have to do with peace? And as their time unfolded, they learned that fighting and living peacefully were choices on opposite sides.

Mackenzie said, "In this hand, I have fighting. In this hand, I have peace. Hmmm. Sometimes, I choose fighting."

Brianna said, "And sometimes I choose peace."

Then the two girls giggled. But they became silent when they overheard Bart say, "I like fighting. Fighting is better. We should all go to war!"

Tony tried to reason with Bart explaining, "But most of the time, when we have gone to war, the argument between the countries could have been settled peacefully."

"But war is better. We can just go in and kill everyone and everything," Bart said. "Then, we can just go in and take over their land and make it peaceful."

Tony and Bart continued their discussion until Tony decided that he would just agree to disagree.

Brianna and Mackenzie thought about what they had heard and made quilt squares for the Peace Quilt. Brianna made a world. Mackenzie drew a chalice. Then, they made prayer flags for peace and hung them on the trees in the church yard.

At the end of the morning, Brianna said to Mackenzie, "Let's always be peaceful."

SPIN, SPIN, SPIN AND THE THREAD FLOWS!
(FROM THE GREEK MYTH OF *THE WEAVING CONTEST* OR *THE STORY OF ARACHNE*)

Spin, spin, spin! Whorl, whorl, whorl! Thwack, thwack, thwack! Sing, sing, sing! Click, click, click! Shwoosh, shwoosh, shwoosh! The weaving sounds waft out over Lydia, where Arachne lives with her shepherd father, who is known for his beautifully dyed crimson wool. The crimson color was not so much red and not so much purple, but somewhere in between.

As the shuttle flows through the warp, the song Arachne weaves on her loom can be heard in the woods where the wood nymphs live and down in the river where the river nymphs live. And curious to see what Arachne is weaving, the nymphs come to peek at her work, leaving their own work to marvel at the brilliant designs.

It shouldn't be surprising that Arachne was captivated by the perpetual magic of raw wool and silk. It shouldn't be surprising that she took to dyeing enchanted colors and found great pleasure in weaving beautiful cloth. But since Arachne had no mother to give her guidance, even the most experienced artisans gasped at the grace and fineness with which Arachne filled her spindle with brilliantly colored thread. When Arachne was not weaving, she spent time among her father's dye pots and raw wool and learning the art of dyeing and spinning.

Arachne spent most of her days in front of her weaving loom. And like most young girls, learned to weave from the other weavers in the village.

Spin, spin, spin! Arachne spun the finest wool. Spin, spin, spin! Arachne spun the finest silk. Whorl, whorl, whorl went the spindle through the weft. Thwack, thwack, thwack went the beater on the threads. Sing, sing, sing went the loom as Arachne's pattern began to form into rhythmic colors flowing in and out and all around her like a multi-colored cloud of fluff.

When Arachne stopped her work, the villagers gasped and crowded in to see. Some of her tapestries were so brilliant and bright that they were hard to look at. Many were filled with designs so intricate and perfect, many thought they must have come from (the Goddess of Weaving) Athena's own loom. But Arachne would laugh them off and say, "these are my own creations. Athena does not weave them, mine are better than Athena's.

The other village women would warn her not to be so bold, but Arachne would shrug them off and tell them of her visions. But the truth is that Athena instructed her in the skills and art of weaving in her dreams. Arachne's knowledge and perceptions changed through this instruction. She began to see not only her work but the world as if it were also a tapestry in progress curving around a great loom. She understood that there were ways in which the world also could be woven more cleverly, and more magnificently. But this led Arachne to re-pattern the world she lived in, as well as Athena's world of Gods and Goddesses in Mt. Olympia.

This new sensuality of creation filled Arachne and consumed her dreams, her weaving, and all thoughts. And as her dreams and thoughts were woven into her weaving designs, the rhythms of the warp and the weft sang lengths of finished fabrics through her hands as the rhythms ran through her life blood and her soul. She wove herself from young girl to young woman holding the brilliantly dyed threads with just enough tension so they flew through the warp with perfectly even tension. All the while, Arachne's rhythms sang out the same rhythms of wisdom that came from the one source she denied: the Goddess Athena.

One day while Arachne was immersed in the patterns, curves, and colors of her inner world and her loom sang out clearly over Lydia, an elderly woman passed by and stopped to see the tapestry. Arachne was used to such admiration. But the old woman admonished her, saying, "You silly little fool, no one dares to weave like the Goddess Athena. Don't you know that the ribbon that lies between the human realm and the Goddess and God realm was placed there for a reason? If you weave like this, you must honor her and give her praises."

Now, Arachne committed the gravest error of all errors. While some believe that Arachne was just too absorbed in her work to understand how arrogant she was, but Arachne's words held no misunderstanding. She clearly retorted, "Be gone, you silly old fool. I don't see Athena complaining."

And at that very moment, Arachne may have seen her error, as the elderly woman transformed herself into Athena and said, "I am she. Let us see just who is the better weaver, shall we? And the judges can be the people of Lydia."

Arachne agreed to the contest. And so, the looms were set up and the mortal and immortal women seated at their looms readied at the break of dawn. Both looms sang with the threads and patterns speedily whorling into fabric as the villagers, the wood and river nymphs, and the Gods and Goddesses of Mt. Olympia looked on.

The patterns of each were brilliant, no doubt. But all who understood the contest knew that besting a God or Goddess could be deadly. As for the villagers of Lydia posing as judges, well, they never had to come head to head with Athena. For as surely as Athena was the Goddess of Weaving, Athena judged her own work in comparison with Arachne's.

"Your stitch patterns are perfect," said Athena. "Why, you've devised some that I have not even thought of or revealed. How did you accomplish such a thing? Which God has given you favors?"

Arachne's responded stuttering, "I – I – You taught me."

"I did no such thing!" bellowed the Goddess. "Colors, such as these, are not permitted to mortals. Where did you find them? On Mt. Olympia? Are they my father's?"

Arachne answered boldly that she herself had spun and dyed the threads. With this, Athena went into a rage and ripped the tapestry. And perhaps, she would have even ended Arachne's life, but at that point, Arachne was overcome by shame. Athena took pity upon her. Instead, she told Arachne that her punishment would be to spin and weave the most beautiful tapestries for the rest of her life while hanging from them! And with that, Athena shrank Arachne's head and bloated her belly with an amazing gift of producing her own silk threads. She also gave her eight arms and named her spider. And thus, a new species arrived on earth. One that can weave the most magnificent weavings in the most gossamer splendor! Spin, spin,

spin and the thread flows to infinity, enough to weave the universe or the awesome tapestry of the garden spider.

As knitters, weavers, crocheters and other needle workers like Arachne, we have the natural ability to see other pieces to a pattern or how to adapt an existing pattern more truthfully or useful to our needs. By defying Athena, Arachne gained immortality, power and influence. She embodies spider magic, which we understand through other myths, such as the Native American Spider Grandmother, are capable of creating the universe, as we;; as, all that is sacred and life giving. Arachnids are capable of laying seven hundred eggs a year! In terms of human creativity, that is probably equal to an infinite number of creative birthing of projects that are woven, knit, crocheted or otherwise the result of needle work.

SILENCE IS MORE THAN JUST NOT SPEAKING

When Zander visited his grandmother, he had to be silent every morning. When he woke up each day, he would go to Grandma and she would hug him. Then, Grandma would go about her kitchen chores while Zander made his bed, brushed his teeth and dressed for the day.

Zander read his books, drew some pictures and sat in the grass outside as he watched Grandma do her morning Tai Chi and greet the day. Sometimes Zander would do Tai Chi with Grandma. And sometimes, he would just watch all the trees bend in the wind and how the flowers seemed to do Tai Chi, as well. Sometimes a squirrel would run across the yard and climb a tree.

At first, it seemed like the morning would never end. Grandma seemed to enjoy her silence. But it took Zander awhile to appreciate it.

Grandma said, "Being silent for the morning helps me focus on my spirit…my soul. There are many ways to pray. The monks at the monasteries tend to live in silence so they can devote their souls to God in reverent focus on the good works they do."

But Zander often got bored with being silent. He had brought his electronic games with him. Grandma said that the games made noise and were not in the spirit of being silent.

"Nine-year-old boys aren't silent," said Zander the second day of his visit.

"Yes, they can be," said Grandma giving Zander a look that made him know that he would begin to enjoy it or endure it for his three-week visit.

Grandma taught Zander how to smudge himself in the Native American traditions and honor the four directions. She taught him to listen to the wind, the earth, the water and the fire. Zander began to understand how to listen to the rocks and trees.

Grandma told him all about Native American spiritual traditions and Zen Buddhism. She told him that it was important to develop a spiritual practice.

A Spider, Some Thread, and a Labyrinth Walk

Zander remembered hearing this at his church. He also remembered lighting a candle and saying some words with all the other people in the sanctuary. But he had never remembered being silent for so long.

Zander often helped Grandma bake the bread to sell. He liked kneading the dough. He helped her take the bread out of the oven. And when the loaves were cool, he helped wrap them in clear plastic bags. He even helped deliver them to her customers.

Grandma's bread was very good. He was proud that his grandmother baked and sold her bread. He felt good when he helped her.

By the beginning of the third week of Zander's visit, he no longer played with his toys that he had brought or read his books during his Grandmother's morning silent rituals. Instead, Zander was spending his time in deep quiet. He liked the smudging and the sacred feeling afterward. He liked the rituals of the Native American spiritual traditions. And though Tai Chi looked cool, he wasn't sure he understood the ideas of Zen Buddhism and whether the two went together. Besides, Tai Chi looked too much like Tae Kwon Do and that was meant for fighting! Zander did know that he was a pacifist, which means that he likes peace not fighting.

The quietness made Zander feel connected to the earth. And though God wasn't a concept that he totally understood, he knew that he did not have to define God as any particular entity. He could feel the awe of something bigger than him like God, an energy source or whatever.

Without naming it, Zander could tap into that cosmic source and feel connected and safe in the quiet place within. He didn't have to know everything about these spiritual traditions to try them out. It was then that Zander understood: Silence is more than just not speaking.

ARIADNE'S THREAD
(ADAPTED FROM GREEK MYTHOLOGY)

While this story is told in many ways, it is set on the island of Crete where King Minos, [*the son of Zeus* (Zeus is always seen as a bull) *and Eruopa*] has married Pasiphae, a daughter of the sun-god Helios. Since King Minos wants to build his bride an elaborate castle fit for the daughter of Helios, he searches for an appropriate person to build such a thing.

Daedalus, an Athenian architect and inventor, is summoned to Crete where King Minos decides that Daedalus, indeed, can build what he wants. Daedalus built King Minos and Queen Pasiphae a magnificent palace just as King Minos had instructed. And since the Cretans worshipped the bull as Zeus, horns of gold in the shape of a bull adorned the roof. This pleased Zeus. But Crete was an island, so it was surrounded by Poseidon's sea. The Sea God Poseidon wanted his own recognition, so he sent King Minos and Queen Pasiphae a white bull from the sea and ordered it sacrificed in his honor.

Queen Pasiphae, however, was quite taken by the bull and refused to allow the sacrifice. Instead, she asked Daedalus to build her a cow in which she could hide. Queen Pasiphae courted the white bull, who became her lover. Not long after she gave birth to a monster, the Minotaur. There are those who believe that Poseidon was angry with her for her failure to obey his wishes and caused her to give birth to the monster instead of King Mino's firstborn son.

Since the Minotaur supposedly only ate human flesh, the monster was not allowed to go free. Yet, King Minos did not have the Minotaur killed, which many say indicates his compassion for his wife's monster offspring. Others say it was recognition of the king's own parenthood. But for whatever reason, the Minotaur existed and must be kept imprisoned to protect the people of Crete. King Minos asked Daedalus to construct the prison.

This prison was in the shape of what we now might call a "Seed" or "Ariadne's Thread" pattern labyrinth. The center of the labyrinth was where the Minotaur lived as a prisoner. There was only one way in and no way out, so the people of Crete saw it. People were sent into the labyrinth to feed the Minotaur. It was believed that once the people crossed the gate into the labyrinth, they lost their way or made their way to the Minotaur who ate them. Although the design was not a maze as we understand them today with wrong turns, it was confusing to the Cretans and it successfully kept the monster imprisoned. There were many rooms and passageways, so the Cretans believed.

Fear was also at work on those who entered the labyrinth, because when the Minotaur was hungry, he bellowed loudly. In fact, he was so loud that the entire palace shook. To keep the Minotaur in food, King Minos had to go to war and feed the prisoners of war to the Minotaur.

One of his sons visited Athens and was accidentally killed, King Minos then required Athens to supply seven maidens and seven male youths to be sacrificed to the Minotaur every nine years. Otherwise, King Minos would destroy Athens. King Aegeus of Athens having no children had nothing to lose and agreed to the terms. The Athenians were not happy with his arrangement, but many years passed and King Aegeus began to grow old.

Meanwhile, a young man named Theseus was destroying all the monsters and highwaymen that crossed his path. Theseus was from Troezen. Now, it happens that many years before, King Aegeus had secretly married Princess Aethra from Troezen, but he never brought her to Athens. He did, however, ask her to bear him a son that would grow up strong enough to lift the boulder under which he hid his sword and golden sandals. But King Aegeus had not seen Aethra for many years.

When Theseus arrived in Athens, he went straight to the king's palace and stood before the King with sandals and sword in hand. The king happily embraced Theseus as his son and the rightful heir to the throne of Athens. He was, in fact, a hero for the Athenians, because he wanted to end the victims of the Minotaur and took one of the youths' places that was scheduled to sail to Crete. He told King Aegeus that he would sail with black sails to Crete and return with white sails as a signal of his success.

The ship arrived in Crete and all fourteen young Athenians were locked in the dungeon. As it happens, King Minos had a lovely daughter, named Ariadne. She was as beautiful as was Theseus handsome. However, Theseus was locked away in her father's dungeon, but she was not happy with this. She went to Daedalus and begged him to help save Theseus. Daedalus gave Ariadne a magic ball of thread. She was instructed to take Theseus to the gate of the labyrinth, tie one end of the thread to the gate so he would find his way back and give him the ball. He was to roll the ball of thread ahead of him and once he found the Minotaur and did his deed, then he could follow the thread back out.

Ariadne made Theseus promise to marry her and carry her away with him if she helped him. Theseus gladly agreed and Ariadne gave him her ball of thread. He rolled the thread and found the Minotaur, who was surprised by Theseus and thus easily overpowered. In fact, Theseus is said to have killed the Minotaur with his bare hands. After killing the monster, he followed Ariadne's "thread" back to the entrance. Together, they freed the other Athenian prisoners and set sail for Athens. Before sailing, of course, they bore holes in all of King Minos' ships to ensure that they would not be pursued.

Thus, the labyrinth has been named after Ariadne and her thread. But the story does not end here. Dionysus, one of the Olympian gods, had wanted Ariadne for his own bride. And since Theseus was not a god, he could not oppose him. At the island of Naxos, Theseus sent everyone ashore for a rest. Ariadne fell into a deep sleep. When she awoke, Theseus was gone. Ariadne was quite sad and wept.

Soon, however, Dionysus arrived and dried her tears. She married Dionysus and they had many sons that became kings of the surrounding islands.

Back to Daedalus. His fate, however, was not so sweet. King Minos knew that he had helped Theseus unravel the mystery of the labyrinth. Therefore, he imprisoned Daedalus in the palace. Later, Daedalus built two sets of wings so that he and his son, Icarus, could fly out of the palace. This, they did, but Icarus flew too close to the sun, which melted the wax that held the wings together. He plunged to his death in the sea.

A Spider, Some Thread, and a Labyrinth Walk

SOPHIA'S MANY-COLORED COAT
(AN ORIGINAL TALE CREATED FROM SCRIPTURES AND MYTHOLOGIES)

Before the earth was earth and the heavens were heavens, Sophia walked with God. When God created the heavens and the earth and all that dwell above and below, Sophia was at His side. She was His spouse, His loved one, His helpful craftsperson. Sophia was sometimes called Wisdom, Hochma or Tree of Life in many of the Bible stories.

Sophia was in the Garden of Eden when Adam and Lilith and Adam and Eve lived there, because she was the Mother creator. While God created heaven and earth, it was Sophia who breathed life into being. She gave birth to Adam and Lilith, the plants, the trees, the birds, the fish and the animals that walked the earth. Even as God created the light and the darkness, She created the sun and moon.

Unlike the Tree of Knowledge, a deer, a bird or fish, Sophia took many forms. She was what we now might call a shape-shifter, because She has visited us in many forms. She walked as easily among people as She did among animals or plants.

Sophia has been part of all living things in the past, present and future. Scientists have said that all of life comes from the same source or that life can be traced to the primordial sea. We all have a similar genetic makeup that makes corn and humans somehow related. Since Sophia is our teacher, we must respect Her in all forms. One way to respect Her is to respect the earth, the animals and the plants as if they are as sacred as She.

Sophia says, "A generation goes, and a generation comes, but the earth remains forever." She offers herself as the Tree of Life, so that people can partake of Her fruit (Wisdom) for She knows all. That is…whatever there is to know, Sophia has given us the power to know and understand. Sophia comes to us when we ask Her. She gives us the knowledge that we need or want. She keeps us safe, like a mother or grandmother watching over a child.

In the Garden of Eden, Sophia was the Tree of Knowledge. When Moses saw the "Burning Bush," it was Sophia speaking to him. And when the Red Sea parted to let Moses and his people pass, it was Sophia who was the sea. She is the land we walk on. Many have called her Mother Earth. She is also Spider Grandmother and Changing Woman. And when Jesus was born in Bethlehem, She was the Angel that appeared to the shepherds. She told them of the importance of Jesus' birth. And when He was born, She was with Him. She helped Jesus become the fisher of men. She was His constant companion as He wandered for 40 days in the forest. As He was being tempted, Sophia was with Him to advise Him.

In the Garden of Gethsemane, Sophia held Jesus' hand as He was arrested. Even as He hung on the cross, Sophia was at His side, for She was a part of Him even as He was a part of Her. And when He told His followers of the Holy Spirit that had always been with them, He told them of Sophia. She is His mother, His grandmother, His creator, His advisor, His challenger, His comforter, His inspiration for changing and reforming the understanding of man and womankind.

Sophia is the woman with the many-colored coat. Like the chameleon, it changes colors to match the need. Whether we are black or white or red or yellow or green like the greenest grass, we are Sophia's child. She also tells us through her own diversity that we are all connected. Her chameleon nature of changing colors extends to her shape, as well. Today, she may appear to you as a tree, but tomorrow, she may human or fish. Sophia walks the earth in her many-colored coat and speaks to us through a woman or a man, sometimes as a bird or animal, possibly even in our dreams.

She is the Holy Spirit of Jesus and God. Sophia built her house and sent out Her servant girls to call from the highest places in town: "Come, eat of my bread and drink of the wine I have mixed." She beacons to those who are hungry for wisdom and knowledge of life to come and eat with Her, take Her fruit, and learn from Her words for Sophia is wisdom personified.

Even before God created the universe, there was the Word. And the Word was holy. Even then, Sophia (Wisdom) was the Word. Sophia is sacred not unlike the sacred word of God, because She is the Word and She is Wisdom and the Tree of Life and the animals in the forest and the fish in the sea and the birds that fly in the air. She is your neighbor and your friend. Sophia is life. And for those who love life, it is said that they, too, must love Sophia.

A Spider, Some Thread, and a Labyrinth Walk

A friend once told me about a persistent woman, a stranger, who spoke to her in a grocery store. But my friend was skeptical, so the woman came to her on every aisle to speak her message. This messenger was Sophia. On another day, Sophia was a crow that refused to be ignored.

For me, Sophia has been a spirit guide taking the form of a hawk, a mouse, and many Goddesses. She takes over my fingers on the keyboard or my pen on the paper to write Her words, tell Her stories, or express Her wisdom.

When Luisah Teish talks about Sophia, she talks about being led by her big toe, because her Sophia looks like Yemaya. Luisah speaks about thinking to go one place and having her car exit and drive her to another.

Sophia is the force behind our subconscious thoughts. She speaks to our intuition and comes to us in dreams. If we trust Her, we find not only where we need to be but what it is we need to learn. Living is learning. And as we learn, we find ourselves being wrapped in Sophia's multi-colored coat with all its shades and shapes.

When the ancient peoples of our world began to communicate and wonder, they first began to ask themselves: How did we become? But what they really were asking is not how did they come to be where they were or who they were but how they became the species that we now call human. The question of how we came to be our species has stumped humans for many years. It is one of the greatest mysteries. And though we may answer some of the questions, we—scientists, theologians, philosophers, storytellers and others (probably even the king's horses, as well)—cannot answer that question with any absolute facts.

Throughout the centuries, the storytellers of the many cultures gave the different people their stories. But though the stories vary widely, it is Sophia who masquerades as Changing Woman or Spider Grandmother, the Native American creator of the seasons, the earth and the universe. It is Sophia who comes as Selu Corn Woman, the Native American goddess of corn, who teaches the people how to tend the corn and harvest it for their food. It is Sophia in her many-colored coat who comes as Yemaya, Neptune, Poseidon, Juno or even Hera, the goddess or god of the sea and is seen as the nurturing mother figure who loves the people. Of course, Poseidon, the sea god or ocean, can also be quite volatile, but this, too, is part of Sophia. As Sophia's many-colored coat gets swirled and swirled, the heavens roil with Oya's angry, changing winds, the thunder. And as the fire spits from deep inside Her bosom, She is Pele. But as the gentle spring flower blooms, Sophia's many-colored coat reveals Her as the love figure Venus, Aphrodite or Oshun.

The earth is filled with many colors from greys to browns to blues to greens and pinks and reds and violets or even more. It is in this many-colored coat that Sophia comes to us as Mother earth or Gaea, Ala or Odudua. And as the rainbow shoots across the sky in its many splendor of colors, it is Sophia, the rainbow Goddess, Mercury or Mars. But as Ares or Damballah or Pandora's curiosity, Sophia comes to teach us the many lessons of life. She is also Amaterasu, the sun, when She hides in Her cave and darkness comes to the people. Likewise, it is Sophia who comes to us as Persephone and Demeter to explain our seasons.

But whether Sophia is the rain in the middle of a drought that quenches the thirst and cools the air or the sun that warms us on a cold, icy day, She is celestial, spiritual and mythological. For those that seek Her, there is great wealth—not as in gold or silver or other exchangeable currency but in understanding, knowledge and true wisdom that she keeps in her coat of many colors. She has always been with us, but Her stories have been often been well hidden. And though She acts as a link between matriarch and patriarch perceptions, it is wise to see how easily She flows in either view. Because Sophia has been Jesus, the man teacher, God, god and Goddess, she is more than mere woman. Sophia is the balancer that equals out that which may seem tipped to one side or the other between race, genders and species.

When you speak to the old woman sitting on her porch smiling, Sophia has greeted you. But if the old woman should yell at you, you may have received Sophia's (Wisdom) lesson. Sophia is the lullabye your mother sang to you in your cradle. She is the comforter, but she does not keep you comfortable. To know Sophia is to keep changing and growing. She is so much a part of everything and everyone, you might say She is the thread, the silk, or the web that holds our interconnected lives together. She is the fabric of time and the emptiness of space.

The stories yet unwritten, unspoken and unsaid are still a part of Sophia. Just as the knowledge yet uncovered is a part of Her wisdom yet to be revealed. Those things—events and every day occurrences—that have yet to come are part of Her. Because, you see, Sophia is also the seeds that have yet to grow, while simultaneously being those that are already sown. As you reap your harvest, She has sown new crops for you to harvest. And when the stories are ready for the telling, those, too, will She deliver to Her messengers. And because Sophia is the Tree of Life, Her fruit is sweet, yet bitter. She reveals both good and bad. And life is full of both. Life is full of Sophia's multi-colored wisdom.

Just as our ancient ancestors found stories to explain their circumstances, we have stories that we tell. They are the models for our life. But as the generations pass, we have need for new models when the old ones cease to work for us. Sophia is the source of all knowledge, models and stories for she is Wisdom.

The African story of Anansi, the tiny spider who gained all the stories from the Sky god, tells us how the stories first came to the people. Sophia teaches us through many stories and She is found in all places. Anansi's stories are Her stories just as this story is Hers. She tells us to listen to all the stories and take from them the knowledge that we can use. But Sophia also teaches us that it is not enough to just listen to the stories, we must learn from Her what is important and how to use it in our lives.

Sophia requires us to commit to Her and be with Her daily. Only through this daily contact can we learn what is important in life. Sophia does not require that we are priests or ministers or that we become scholars on Her behalf. But we must trust Her.

Our ancestors learned from Her and trusted Her in Her many colors, shapes and names from Hecate to White Buffalo Calf Woman to God and Jesus and the Rainbow Snake of the Aborigines. Her face is the face of ancient goddesses, Jesus, God and angels. Sophia requires only that you seek Her with your soul. She is Black to those who are Black and Red to those who are Red, but Her coat is full of all the colors of the Universe. She will wrap you in that coat, so that you, too, can understand all the colors of the Universe.

A Spider, Some Thread, and a Labyrinth Walk

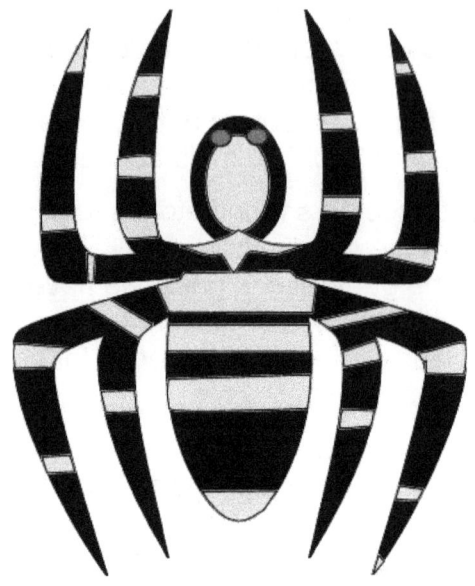

Bramble of Pincup Springs

Bramble is a garden spider, who lives at Pincup Springs near the East window of the church on Bramble Road. She likes her window, because the meditation garden is below her. "All is peaceful," Bramble always boasts, "because I live in a church garden."

But all that changed when the church hired Griffo Frogmorton to be the gardener. Rev. Lotho Boggs hired the man after old man Needles Whitcomb got too old to tend the garden. But Griffo was not as gentle as Needles and he probably had better eyesight, so he saw Bramble's beautifully spun web one Spring morning just before the dew had evaporated.

Griffo plucked one end of her web and might have gotten more had he not gotten distracted by Ruby Grubb's tiny dog, Peanut, who began to yap like a mad dog. Ruby shushed her dog and Griffo returned to weeding.

It happened that Griffo was weeding under Bramble's web. She had gone to a lot of trouble to spin this web from the window to a nearby tree. It was almost three feet in diameter. Her black-and-yellow body had had a workout that morning going up and down and across and around until she had spun the most delicate of webs.

As the wind blew, her entire web would gently rock. It had a calming affect on Bramble. Still, she could bear no more tampering of her web. So when Griffo looked in her direction, she began giving him what for! Of course, Bramble was just a garden spider and Griffo did not even hear her. As far he and most humans were concerned, spiders made no sounds and were incapable of communication.

Only a miracle could change this perception and that was a rather large task for a small arachnid. But even small creatures are capable of causing very large transformations in the web of all existence. And that is what she did!

First, Bramble left her window and sat upon a bench in the meditation garden below. She sat there for a very long time. And while most humans did not know spiders meditated that is what she was doing. It was there that her path became quite clear to her.

A Spider, Some Thread, and a Labyrinth Walk

While humans debated the existence of God and whether Jesus performed miracles and if there really was such a thing as heaven and hell or life after death or what religion was better than another, spiders understood the universal truth of nature. Bramble knew that her great, great, great, great, great, great-grandmother had been the spider grandmother of Native American lore. So as all her mothers before her, Bramble asked the Great Spider Grandmother to grant her a miracle so that she could talk to humans for one day.

As it happened, the day of Bramble's miracle was an Easter morning when all the children were out hunting Easter Eggs and Rev. Boggs was talking about the miracles of Spring and the transformations that happen as a result of the miracles. Bramble had listened well during his sermon. But being the small creature that she was, she waited for all the children and their parents to go home, before she tried out her miracle.

Rev. Boggs was about to leave his church after cleaning up after Sunday morning service, which he did most Sundays.

Bramble cleared her throat, "Uhmmm, uhummm. Uh, Rev. Boggs."

Rev. Boggs looked all around and he did not see anyone. He muttered to himself: "I must be getting senile! I'm beginning to hear strange voices."

"I assure you, sir, you are not hearing strange voices," said Bramble. "You are only hearing the voice of Bramble, the garden spider that lives on the East window above your meditation garden."

With that, Rev. Boggs began to look for her.

"I'm here," she said. "On the door, above the handle…just at your eyelevel."

Sure enough, she was there and Rev. Boggs saw her. But he was having a bit of trouble adjusting to the fact that he was hearing a spider speak.

"Then I'm just going crazy! Because spiders don't talk!" he confessed.

"No, sir," Bramble assured. "You are fine. I have been granted a miracle. And I have chosen it to be to talk with humans."

"That's a strange way to spend a miracle," said Rev. Boggs. "There are so many things you could have asked for."

"And what would those be?" asked Bramble.

"Well, to be something else rather than a spider. To be human with a nice income, I suppose. I don't know. Now that I say this, perhaps you are right…"

"Yes, sir. I suppose there were many things I could have requested. But none of them would have been worthy of a miracle as miraculous as this."

Rev. Boggs agreed with Bramble. And she told him that humans did not respect the work of spiders. She relayed to him that the new gardener, Griffo Frogmorton, had destroyed her precious web. She went on to tell him all the good that spiders of her species did for gardeners, such as eat grasshoppers, aphids, flies and the occasional bee.

"Yet," she pointed out, "Griffo Frogmorton disrespected my existence by destroying my web. Do humans understand the interdependent web of all existence?"

Rev. Boggs assured Bramble that not only did his congregation understand this, but that it was one of the principles that his church held sacred.

Bramble convinced Rev. Boggs to call Griffo Frogmorton for a meeting. "I will only be able to communicate with humans for this day only," she said when Rev. Boggs pointed out that it was a holiday for humans.

"Very well," he agreed, "A miracle should not go unused to its fullest."

Griffo, Rev. Boggs and Bramble sat in Rev. Boggs' office and discussed how she had been discriminated against. Griffo apologized. And together the three of them came to some agreements.

Neither Griffo nor Rev. Boggs ever disrespected another spider, whether it was a garden spider or another species. And Rev. Boggs often told this story of Bramble of Pincup Springs and her miracle.

PEACE BEGINS WITH ME

Mahalia Minerva wanted world peace. She knew that there were soldiers fighting in Iraq and Afghanistan. She had learned that presidents and law makers felt fighting would eventually bring peace. She had learned about the day the towers fell in 2001 when terrorists flew planes into New York's World Trade Center.

But she wondered how fighting could bring peace? Her principal had talked to their entire student body about how fighting did not bring about peaceful behavior. Arguments that involved any violence or fighting would only bring on more violence.

Mahalia Minerva was 12 years old and had been interested in peace since she was seven or eight. She knew that people had all sorts of disagreements and that sometimes people fought instead of making peace. But Mahalia Minerva thought that there must be a way for everyone in every place from Mozambique to Seattle, Washington, to live peacefully.

She talked to her mother, her father and her brother. She talked to her teachers at church and at school. She talked to her minister and the director of their religious education program. And the message that she heard over and over was that "peace begins with me."

Mahalia Minerva thought and thought and thought. The idea of peace beginning with her was a hard idea. Although it sounded sort of simple, she knew it wasn't going to be easy. And so, it proved to be very difficult, indeed!

Mahalia's best friend, Freda Farrah worked in the library during her study hall. The librarian was concerned because <u>Pastachio Pace's Peace Parade</u> was missing. The records indicated that it had not been checked out. Freda looked through all the books to be reshelved, but she did not turn up the book. Freda sent a text to Bunny Bird that said: "<u>Pastachio Pace's Peace Parade</u> is missing and I know you took it!"

Bunny texted back: "It wasn't me! I don't even know that book! I think it is Talbot Tegwen's favorite book."

A Spider, Some Thread, and a Labyrinth Walk

Freda texted Talbot: "Pastachio Pace's Peace Parade is missing and I know you took it!"

Talbot texted back: "Not me! I don't have it!"

Pretty soon, Freda had accused half of the 7th grade class of taking the book. Everyone was mad at Freda. After school, they all came to find her. Instead of apologizing, Freda said, "Well, one of you has Pastachio Pace's Peace Parade!"

Elmer Ely threw the first punch. Priscilla Pomona, who was taller and bigger than even the biggest boy in the class, pinned Freda to the wall and said, "so what's it to you if someone pinched Pastachio Pace's Peace Parade! We're going to teach you a lesson in minding your own business." Then, she punched Freda in the stomach.

That's when Mahalia finally pushed through the crowd and saw what was happening. "STOP!" she cried. "Peace begins with each of us. We have to find a peaceful solution!"

Priscilla yelled angrily, "Yeah, and what's it to you?"

"To find a peaceful solution!" Mahalia retorted. "Do you want to go to jail?"

Mr. Willoughby had made it through the crowd as well and waited to hear Priscilla's answer.

"I won't go to jail! You're just saying that to get me to stop," Priscilla said.

Mr. Willoughby took over, "Priscilla, you come with me to my office."

Priscilla followed.

Meanwhile, Mahalia checked on Freda. "Are you alright?"

"I think so!" said Freda.

"What did you do to Priscilla? You know you should always stay away from her," said Mahalia.

"I guess I asked for this!" said Freda. "I was just trying to find a book that someone took from the library."

"So what did you do?" asked Mahalia.

Freda told Mahalia everything.

"No wonder half of the school was out here!" Mahalia exclaimed. "You may have some apologies to make."

Freda said, "I suppose so."

"And you'll probably have to talk to Mr. Willoughby, as well."

Mr. Willoughby walked up about this time. "So…I hear you've been accusing everyone of taking a book from the library."

"Yes," said Freda.

"Let's go talk about it in my office to talk," Mr. Willoughby said.

"Remember," said Mahalia, "Peace begins with me…and you…and everyone! We all have to be peaceful for there to be peace in the world!"

Mr. Willoughby smiled, "Those are wise words! Too bad your friend, here, didn't think of that before she started texting!"

THE STAR KEEPER

Once upon a time long ago in a time before the earth was orderly with a sun that shone each day and a moon and stars that shone each night, there was a Star Keeper. The Star Keeper was very proud of the stars. In fact, he was so proud of his stars that he kept them hidden in a star-shaped box so that none of them would be lost.

Each day the Star Keeper would take out the stars and count them and polish them to keep them bright. The stars were his joy. And each day he would put them back in the star-shaped box.

Now as time passed and the world was beginning to get organized, the Star Keeper noticed that the Sun would get tired and go to sleep every now and then. During this time, the beings on the earth would wish for a bit of brightness so that their night would not be so dark.

The Star Keeper heard their wish, but he was worried that someone might want his stars. After all, they did shine quite nicely. However, the Star Keeper did not want to share his stars with anyone. They were his to care for and they were his to keep. He quit opening the box each day, so that not one of his stars could get lost.

But the stars missed their daily routine of being polished and counted. The Star Keeper carried them around and the stars rubbed together inside the box causing a sparkly dust to appear all around the stars.

The dust easily lit up the inside of the box and the stars realized that they were being trapped against their wishes. One day while the Star Keeper was eating his lunch, he tipped the box and spilled some of the star dust out into the dark night sky. The star dust swirled and whirled and found a place to be. It wasn't a lot of light, but the beings on the earth noticed. They were "ooo-ing" and "ahhh-ing" and it made the Star Keeper feel sad that he still kept the stars in his star-shaped box. So, he flung the lid off the box and scattered the stars all over the night sky.

The stars were so happy that they sparkled brighter than they had ever sparkled before. And the Star Keeper learned to share his joy with all the beings on the earth. And since that day, the beings have said that if you can find some star dust, your wish will surely come true.

As for the Star Keeper, he learned to respect all beings, including the stars.

MRS. KOROVSKI'S MAGICAL BUTTERFLY GARDEN

Some people call Mrs. Korovski crazy. Some people call her weird or strange. All my friends cross to the other side of the street, because they're afraid that she might talk to them. But I live right next door to her and my mother thinks it would be rude not to talk to her.

Her place is really colorful. Out front she has all these twirly things that blow in the wind. Each one is different and very bright in color. And there are wind chimes everywhere!

I really don't mind talking to Mrs. Korovski, even when she starts talking about her dead husband or when she starts talking to the plants and insects...and the butterflies in her garden. I'll tell you a secret: Mrs. Korovski's garden is a magical butterfly garden.

Mrs. Korovski showed me a tiny caterpillar just a few weeks ago. And then, she showed me one in a cocoon. It looked a lot like a mummy in the museum, but then...just when I thought it was surely dead, out came the most gorgeous butterfly you have ever seen.

Actually, Mrs. Korovski has a garden of butterflies among her flowers. The Black Swallowtail ate carrots and celery when it was a caterpillar, but now it likes the clover and thistle. The Tiger Swallowtail ate wild cherry as a caterpillar and now enjoys the lilacs and the honeysuckle.

I began to count the different butterflies. I think I lost count at 23. Mrs. Korovski says that there are hundreds of different types of butterflies around the world and each of them like a different type of plant. She says that butterflies are as different as people!

My mother says that butterflies are flaws in nature, because they are way more colorful than they need to be. But I also learned that color is what attracts butterflies to certain plants.

You know, Mrs. Korovski's garden looks like some sort of weird, colorful, chaotic mistake like maybe when you leave your crayons out in the sun too long. But when you look inside the garden, you find out that every plant is there for some butterfly. I think it's magical and sacred!

A Spider, Some Thread, and a Labyrinth Walk

It's one of those places you can just sit down and watch and watch and watch. It isn't television or a movie or a video game, but I think it's much more fantastic than that.

EILEEN OF SKELLIG BOG
IN THE GARDEN OF TUATHA DE DENANN

When Eileen of Skellig Bog was born, she inherited the gift of light. It was an ancient gift left over from the tribe of Dana (Dawn-a). It was said that Dana was the mother of Tuatha De Danann (Two-a-Day-Dawn-an). And the Goddess Dana was often seen as THE GREAT MARE. As it happened, on the birth day of Eileen of Skellig Bog, a mare appeared at her door.

Eileen had a fairly normal childhood and no one thought about the mare and no one knew about the gift, because the gift was inherited and all those who had come before her who would know of such things were now living in the spirit world.

But magical gifts have a way of teaching all their own. And though it might be just as intriguing to tell you of her studies and with whom Eileen of Skellig Bog learned about the ancient myths, the night is short and the story is long. Let's suffice it to say, she studied all the old texts she could find. And her dreams repeatedly showed her opening the doors to a garden. Even she began to realize that the garden was none other than that of Twatha De Danann that had vanished with her ancient foremothers. And the adventure was in her heart and on her lips. For if she were to live in peace, she knew she must find the secret key to opening those doors.

Behind the doors in Tuatha De Danann, the myths spoke of three magical items sealed in the other world: The SPEAR OF LUGH, the SWORD OF NUADA and the CAULDRON OF DAGDA. Each item held magical powers. Long ago, when people began to disbelieve in Tuatha De Danann or the Tribe of Dana, a wise woman caused the items to fall into this land and be sealed away so that the magic would not be misused by evil people.

Over and over, Eileen of Skellig Bog saw in her dreams the opening of the doors to this world. And she saw herself causing them to open. She did not know what would await her in the Garden of Tuatha De Danann. But it was clear that she, Eileen of Skellig Bog, was destined to open the ancient doors.

A Spider, Some Thread, and a Labyrinth Walk

A wise woman appeared to Eileen just before her 18th birthday. She explained to Eileen of Skellig Bog that she had been given the gift of *light*. Even her name meant *light* and that the gift was meant to be used as a key to open a door.

After more studies, Eileen of Skellig Bog was ready to set out on her adventure of opening the doors to the ancient Garden of Tuatha De Danan. Still, she had no idea what would happen. Her mentors and teachers had cautioned her about being faint at heart and not following through boldly. For once the door was open, if she should waiver; it could shut her inside forever. She must believe with all her heart that she would find what she needed by opening the door. Once open, the adventure was on its way and she must remain sure of herself throughout the adventure.

She learned that Tuatha De Danann was a faerie realm more ancient than Leprechauns and more powerful than Mount Olympus. Her first job was to make a magical FAERY WAND and learn to use it. Then, she had to create a magical SHIELD and SWORD and learn to use them. Along the way, she also had to make a BOOK OF SHADOWS and commit to keeping her dreams and memories to use as an aid in the realm beyond.

As Eileen of Skellig Bog learned to control her inner powers, she began to understand the magical gift of light that she had been given. And when the day was right, she stood in the moonlight repeating the familiar words to create the sacred space from which she would work. She asked the GUARDIANS for strength and boldness.

With her feet planted firmly on the soil, she picked up her FAERY WAND and pointed it skyward. Using words from the OLD TONGUE, she called upon her gift of LIGHT to open the doors of Tuatha De Danann. She whirled the wand in the air and struck it against the earth.

Lightning exploded from the clear starlit sky as if the moon had thrown the bolt like a dart toward the point where she had struck the soil with her WAND. A deep fog filled the air and a ghost wind blew the chilliness in as if the tang of the high seas were upon this inland place.

Again, Eileen raised her WAND and brought it down as if parting the now-thick air. As she moved, she spoke more words. A glowing milk-white light appeared. At first it was dim, but Eileen shut her eyes as it grew brighter and brighter. She remembered that she must not look into the light for the mind could not comprehend the opening of the DOOR BETWEEN THE WORLDS. To look into the light would be to destroy her sight forever.

As bright as the light became, Eileen could feel it on her eyelids. And though her eyes were closed, the light seemed brighter than when she turned her closed eyes toward the sun on a sunny afternoon. She knew she must keep her eyes closed against the brightness.

She suddenly caught the scent of clove and salt in the breeze. The light began to dim. Finally, she knew it was safe to open her eyes. She opened them slowly. Before her hung a shimmer of white fog that blurred the beauty of what lay beyond.

Yet, Eileen trembled with excitement as she carefully stepped into the mist and into the GARDEN OF TUATHA DE DANANN.

Once inside the garden, Eileen could see clearly. It was as if she had stepped inside a drop of water, because the walls of the garden shimmered and appeared to reflect the images inside the garden.

As she looked closer at the flowers, she realized they were not flowers at all but faeries. They were the colors of jewels.

Eileen knew her mission was to find the CAULDRON OF DAGDA. If she could find the CAULDRON and learn its knowledge, then she could retrieve all three magical items. The trick was to find the CAULDRON, learn its knowledge and leave this realm before eating or dancing with the faeries. One who does either is destined to stay in the faerie realm forever.

"Can you tell me where the CAULDRON OF DAGDA lies?" Eileen asked the faeries.

The faeries laughed and flew away. Eileen followed. After awhile, a face of an old woman appeared.

"Are you Dana?" asked Eileen.

The old woman nodded and beckoned her to come and sit with her. "What do you want with the CAULDRON OF DAGDA?" asked the old woman.

"To satisfy my hunger," she answered.

"The food is of another world, it will not fill your belly, daughter," Dana explained.

"Perhaps it can satisfy my hunger for knowledge," suggested Eileen.

Dana asked her a long list of questions, which revealed that she was on a quest to find the cauldron and that Eileen of Skellig Bog had used her gift of LIGHT to open the door to the world. Dana did not seem surprised by any of her answers.

Finally, Dana asked, "Before you can find the cauldron, you must call it by its name.

Eileen answered, "Why it is the CAULDRON OF DAGDA and it's name is THE UNDRY."

The old woman began to fade and in its place was a large cauldron.

But just as Eileen was about to dip her hands into the cauldron to bring out the knowledge that was inside, she remembered that LUGH'S SPEAR would be stuck in the cauldron. Lugh often kept the point of his spear in Dagda's Cauldron to keep the village from going up in flames. The SPEAR was extremely powerful. But had she nicked her hand on the SPEAR, it would have been sudden death for Eileen of Skellig Bog.

Eileen grabbed what she thought would be the handle of the SPEAR and removed it from the cauldron. Having safely removed the SPEAR, Eileen dipped her hands deep into the cauldron and was immediately fulfilled.

Although Eileen was the GUARDIAN of LIGHT and the SPEAR OF LUGH was rightly hers, she knew no mortal ever left the GARDEN OF TUATHA DE DANAN with anything that belonged to the other world.

She returned the SPEAR and vowed she would return to seek its powers and to find the SWORD OF NUADA. But for now, she knew she must return to her own world. If she should stay until the sun came up in the human world, she would be only a prisoner in the faerie realm.

She had found the KNOWLEDGE of the CAULDRON OF DAGDA. It was hers to keep. She would have to return some other time for the other magical items.

Eileen returned to where the white mist hung heavy. As she crossed the threshold into the human world, she knew she had much to learn. After all, what was knowledge if you could not apply it at the right time and place?

She turned to face the DOOR and said, "Blessed Be the Keeper of the Knowledge of the DOOR to the Garden of Tuatha De Denann, may I serve you well."

With that, she bowed and went home. Her adventure was over for the day. Tomorrow, however, would bring new adventures. For she who is the KEEPER OF KNOWLEDGE is often sought to solve many problems, including what to do with more knowledge.

A Spider, Some Thread, and a Labyrinth Walk

ABOUT THE LABYRINTH

Since the beginning of time, women and men have journeyed to other lands or villages and returned changed. And while the pilgrimage or journey was a physical journey for the most part, there were spiritual aspects, which were what actually made the person change. It is believed that the labyrinths found in ancient churches were used to create a pilgrimage or journey experience. However, evidence of the labyrinth is far older than Christianity.

The cloverleaf design also known as the Chartres design, because this design is the design of the one in Chartres Cathedral.

The design in the First Universalist Society's grove was first etched on a small clay tablet from Pylos in approximately 1200 B.C. This same design was also found in Pompeii. This squared off design is generally referred to as the Hopi symbol, Tapu'at or Mother and Child, sometimes it is also called the symbol of Mother Earth.

When the design is rounded rather than squared, it can still be considered the Hopi symbol of Mother Earth. However, it is more often referred to as Ariadne's Thread (See *Ariadne's Thread*), which brings to life the story of the Minotaur, a monster character that is half-man and half-beast. Ariadne is also sometimes referred to as Sophia or Wisdom, the Goddess of Biblical lore. While this story directly relates to the Labyrinth, another story Spider Woman (See *Spider Woman*) relates to the middle of the Labyrinth design, where the (+) plus sign marks the center of the Labyrinth. This same mark of the (+) is claimed by the Christians as the Cross, which is why the Labyrinth has been a religious tool since the Middle Ages. See the section on creating a Labyrinth to see more clearly this symbol that hides within the Labyrinth design. It is not present, however, on the Chartres Labyrinth, which is an 11-rung labyrinth also referred to as the Cloverleaf Labyrinth because of the center that resembles a cloverleaf.

How to Use a Labyrinth?

Through the use of many meditative forms, you can experience the pilgrimage by walking a labyrinth. The goal is not to find Mecca or Jerusalem but to find your internal self: the soul, the deity, and the spirit. The purpose of the pilgrimage was transformational, but many people could not - and still cannot - take a pilgrimage for a variety of reasons.

A labyrinth is simply a pattern with one way in and one way out. It is not a maze with wrong turns. It is similar, but the way in is clear. Usually, you walk to a center point and then out again by the same path. Indoor labyrinths are usually painted directly on the floor's surface or done in tile. Music and candlelight often accompany a walk on the labyrinth. Some labyrinths are formed outside in natural settings. There aren't any right or wrong ways to have a labyrinth.

Why journey on a labyrinth? The labyrinth is believed to have been used by many Christians in place of a pilgrimage to return to Rome. The journey is a spiritual journey. Much like the quest for the Holy Grail, a walk on a labyrinth helps a person get in touch with their most sacred side. One of the first labyrinths was in Crete and was actually designed as a prison for the Minotaur, a half-human, half-bull monster that is probably more legendary than real.

Many churches had labyrinth designs, either large-enough to walk or to decorate the doorway into the church. While there aren't very good explanations of why these exist, it is believed that the labyrinth represented the pilgrimage. A pilgrimage is almost always associated with spiritual growth.

Through the use of many meditative forms, you can experience the pilgrimage that our religious forefathers and foremothers found by simply walking a labyrinth. The goal is not to find Mecca or

Jerusalem but to find your internal self: the soul, the deity, and the spirit. Many people walk very slowly, some walk faster. Some like music and some like silence. Walking a labyrinth is a spiritual experience for many people.

Chakras and the Labyrinth

Many people like walking the labyrinth in connection with their work on charkas.

Layer 1, *red* or *C* note, relates to the first Chakra or the *Physical/Root Chakra*

Layer 2, *orange* or *D* note, relates to the second Chakra or the *Emotional Chakra*

Layer 3, *yellow* or *E* note, relates to the third Chakra or the *Mental Chakra*

Layer 4, green or F note, relates to the fourth Chakra or the Heart Chakra

Layer 5, *blue* or *G* note, relates to the fifth Chakra or the *Throat Chakra*

Layer 6, indigo or A note, relates to the sixth Chakra or Third Eye/Brow Chakra

Layer 7, *violet* or *B* note, relates to the seventh Chakra or the *Crown Chakra*

Center area, white or C note, completes the octave, and relates to the overall aura or white light, often called a healing light/God/Goddess's light

Dancing the Labyrinth

Dancing and playing games on the labyrinth are also ways of accessing our spiritual selves and experiencing the labyrinth. Children love to dance and run the labyrinth, but may not totally understand its spiritual aspects. Dancing, in particular, brings out the spiritual, as well as our inner child. While on the labyrinth, the dances must be limited to the pattern and the walkway spaces. Dancing on uneven labyrinths and many of the natural labyrinths with hard substances as walls can be hazardous or difficult.

However, dancing, in general, can awaken parts of our spirit that our American culture has turned off. In Africa, for example, dancing is an important part of their spiritual heritage. Singing and dancing their history from generation to generation, the native people of Africa keep pace with their culture.

Native Americans traditionally have danced their prayers. Group dancing is still practiced by Native Americans and is considered a sacred art form. Singing and dancing is an integral part of the Native American culture and spirituality.

Just as dancing prayers in African and Native American cultures are common, we can awaken that part of our spirit by participating in spiritual dance. One of the most common dances among spiritual women is the spiral dance. These dances do not look anything like popular dancing. They have nothing to do with male-female dating rituals or popular music. However, at many gatherings of women of faith, chants are sung as snake or spiral dancing is begun.

In our American culture, we don't move. We are stagnant and rigid. As a society, we do not touch or dance unless we are at a "dance" or "music concert." But there is spirituality to be found in dancing. As the Native Americans, Africans and many other indigenous people of the world understand, dancing with our bare feet touching the earth is spiritual, sacred and holy. Perhaps the spirituality comes with the thoughts we hold as we dance. Moving adds an aspect to prayer that cannot be explained but only experienced.

Dancing to drumming; dancing to chants; and dancing and moving to spiritual music is an experience that many women of faith use in various religious and spiritual rituals. Dancing on the labyrinth can be a new awakening, as well.

On the labyrinth, there tends to be a rhythm that you set for walking. You can add foot patterns to your walking, but keep them simple. Dancing the labyrinth should be done as soulfully as walking the labyrinth. It is, after all, a dancing meditation or prayer.

The Labyrinth and Its Meaning

There has been lots of discussion in recent years about just what the Labyrinth was originally designed to do and what meaning it still has in our life today. Many believe its best attributes are as a meditation tool.

The Celtics, however, believed the labyrinth was a key to astral projection or the key to transporting them into the "Otherworld." The best way of describing the "Otherworld" is to describe it as "Between the Worlds" or the "Spirit World." However, many disciplines define it differently, equating the "Otherworld" to a dream state. Yet, others refer to it as a non-physical place. Many might also think of it as an "out of body experience."

In today's world, we see the labyrinth as more of a metaphor on many different levels. Thinking of it as a metaphor for life, we understand that when we reach the middle or the halfway point, we are then on the last half of our journey of life. Walking the labyrinth with these thoughts in mind, one might look at all the successes one has experienced or will experience up to the middle of life, which now sits at about age 50. It is the walking out of the labyrinth and contemplating the end of life that is often the most challenging.

Christians view the labyrinth as a holy object. If you've learned to draw the labyrinth, (See *Creating a Labyrinth*), you'll understand the powerful symbol of the cross within some labyrinth designs. It is for this reason, that Christians today are holding the labyrinth as a sacred event. It is thought that walking the labyrinth is a metaphor for becoming a reborn Christian.

On the other hand, the Celts take this same design and explain the cross that starts the pattern as the Labrys or double-headed ax. The center of the labyrinth represents the womb of the Goddess.

You can see the parallel here is great. Both meanings represent rebirth. The similarities are not great coincidences. Center to the Christian belief system is the rebirth of its members into Christian society. Ancient Celts and new Pagan and Earth-based Spiritual followers understand the power of the life-death-rebirth cycle. Therefore, if walking the labyrinth takes you into the death and rebirth from the Goddess, you have experienced a transformation. Transformation is the goal in Christianity, as well.

Spirals are one of the symbols most closely aligned with the labyrinth. For the most part, a labyrinth design is a glorified spiral. Spirals and other circular patterns can be found in all sorts of nature. See the section on *Mandalas* for more discussion about spirals. Since these patterns occur naturally in nature, it is the contention of many authorities that the labyrinth and its associated spirals are a manifestation of the human to replicate nature. However, others believe that the pattern is key to our universe and that somehow it connects us with all other parts of the universe.

Mathematicians talk about prime numbers as a basic of the universe. But spiritual basics may lie in the spiral patterns of the labyrinth. It is as though all throughout the universe, sentient beings are traveling this same pattern. Maybe it is a communications device or maybe it is simply a way for us to connect in the "Otherworld."

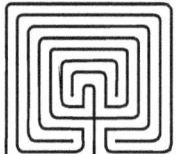

The Labyrinth and the Hopi Symbol

The Hopi or "Mother Earth" pattern is often found in Native American art. The Hopi pattern is also referred to as Tapu'at or Mother and Child. In India, it is also seen as a symbol of birth, because it's seven layers symbolically represented what Middle Age magical notions considered the makeup of a woman's uterus.

Today, the labyrinth remains a symbol of Mother Earth, as well as of birth and rebirth (usually referring to our spiritual birth and rebirth from Mother Earth).

In many of the drawings of the Hopi symbol the plus (+) in the middle of the design is quite prevalent. While Christians take this as the cross, the ancient Hopi saw this as a correlation to their sacred earth and the division of it into the four sectors that Grandmother made when she created the earth. See *Grandmother Spider* story.

The beginnings of the labyrinth, the plus (+) are even more prevalent. Perhaps that is why we see this pattern in African, Mexican, New Zealand and Australian indigenous art. Like many Mandala designs, where nature is reflected, the plus (+) of the labyrinth design can also be found in nature, which might explain why it is found in so many different cultures.

Creating a Labyrinth

The labyrinth is simply a design, a Mandala design. It is pretty much a circle or a spiral with a route to the center. Some labyrinths, however, have been created that are not circles. I walked one once that was in the shape of a hand. Labyrinths can be designed large or small in circles or not.

One labyrinth that is fairly easy to draw is a seven-layered labyrinth, often referred to as the "seed" pattern or "Ariadne's Thread" pattern. This pattern resembles a seed and is started from a simple cross or plus (+) sign. When you add the L-shaped additions and the dots, you are ready to draw your labyrinth. When the walking paths are rounded out more, the shape is more seed-like. The pattern illustrated here, is more squared.

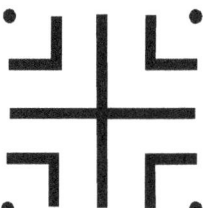

Labyrinth Illustration 1

A Spider, Some Thread, and a Labyrinth Walk P - 60

Connect the lines to draw the labyrinth. Begin at the top of the plus sign. See *Labyrinth illustration 2* and *3*.

The labyrinth of this design is often used in conjunction with work on the chakra system. See *Chapter 15* and the *Chakra* section. Since there are seven chakras, each level is considered equal to one of the chakras. Chakras also have a color and part of the body that they represent. Walking the labyrinth with the chakras in mind is healing.

While other labyrinth designs are more elaborate and provider longer walks, this labyrinth is more flexible and can be fit into smaller spaces. This design will easily fit into a backyard area.

Your first job in laying out a labyrinth is to survey the spot where the labyrinth will go. Since this is a walking activity, you want to make sure that the spot is fairly level, if not, you may have a hard time walking. After you have leveled your area, mark out the spot with rope or heavy string.

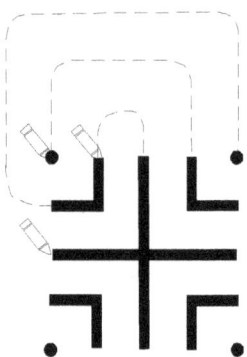

Labyrinth Illustration 2

The labyrinth of this design with a basic 10 inches walk room within the layers takes up approximately 8.33 feet in depth and 9.17 feet in width or 100 inches by 110 inches. The design can be expanded, of course to accommodate a wider walk space. If the design is painted on the floor or on a cement-type surface outdoors, where a person can walk on the walls (the marks between the walking spaces), make the space between the walls 10-inches so most people's feet fit between the walls. However, if you are putting bricks or rocks or that sort of boundary between the layers or rungs of the labyrinth, you need to expand the walking room. While measuring one foot at a time, people's feet are not 10 inches wide. However, if you look at strides and comfortable widths to walk, 10 inches is a minimum size. You can always expand the walking spaces, if your space is larger. When walking with larger numbers of people, you also have to consider the passing room of shoulder to shoulder on the narrow paths.

There develops a sort of *Labyrinth Etiquette* that requires people to walk in silence at their own pace and pass others near a curve. Stepping out of your current path, if necessary, while someone passes, and then resuming your course. If there is a labyrinth director, she or he normally paces people out, so that you aren't on each other's heals.

Some people enjoy walking extremely slowly and others enjoy walking faster. The faster people normally pass the slow ones. But the basic *Labyrinth Etiquette* is to respect each other. Labyrinth walks are normally done as a meditative activity.

With the information given in this section, you can create your own labyrinth. Check out your space, select your materials and go to work! It might be a good idea to practice on paper first. Don't worry if your drawing doesn't look perfect. And when you finish your labyrinth, it may not look absolutely perfect…and that's okay, too. Some of the best labyrinths are imperfect.

To get the measurements just right, you need to make a grid on your paper or flooring. To put it on canvas or other material, you can make a grid with pencil or chalk. Cut a piece of sandpaper to the correct size or use masking tape to put several pieces together to make the right size. Use the sandpaper as a template or pattern for the grid. Lay it down and mark the edges, then lay it down next to the marks and continue until you have laid out a grid. Then you can make your walkways more perfect.

This rounded square design is easier to map out than the traditional "seed" pattern. However, mathematicians, architects, and graphic designers can easily convert this pattern to a more circular design.

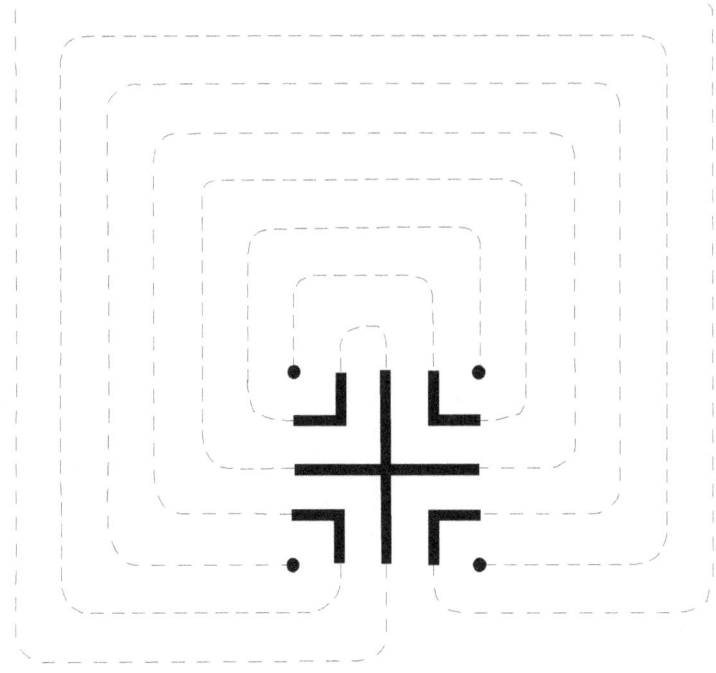

Labyrinth Illustration 3

The squared off pattern creates a HOPI labyrinth design. The Hopis, however, did not use this design as a labyrinth. You may find it in their other art works, because to them, this was a symbol of mother earth or the sacred mother.

While this labyrinth pattern makes a seven-layered labyrinth, the pattern can be extended. By adding more I-shapes and dots to the pattern, it makes more layers.

A Spider, Some Thread, and a Labyrinth Walk P - 63

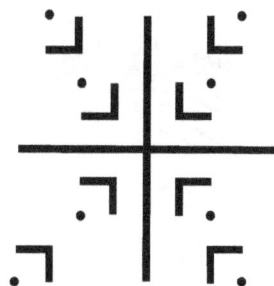

Labyrinth Illustration 4

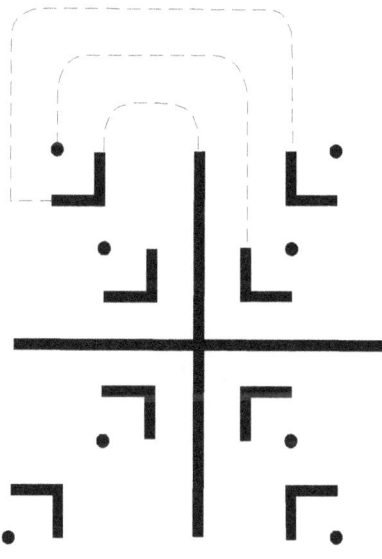

Labyrinth Illustration 5

There are other designs of labyrinths. For example, the most popular design is the CLOVERLEAF design or Chartres labyrinth design. This pattern makes a larger labyrinth, which can accommodate more people.

Cloverleaf Labyrinth

This labyrinth can also be drawn out using some mathematics. But its complexity makes it a bit more of a chore. However, a wonderful Web site explains step by step how to draw both of these labyrinths: http://www.geomancy.org. And the kits to help you create them are available for sale through Grace Cathedral at http://www.gracecathedral.org.

In general, find a central point to whatever your design. Decide how wide your walking lanes will be. The bigger the crowd you expect, the larger the lanes should be. Then design your labyrinth from your center point with the desired width of the lanes.

People have made labyrinths on most surfaces and in a variety of spaces. Virtually no space is too small or too large. You simply adjust your labyrinth to fit your space. If you are using a hard surface, such as cement, you can even use tape to create it. If you want to make it permanent, replace the tape with paint.

The Pilgrimage

Many pilgrimages where spiritual growth occurs are not planned. Some people take a pilgrimage without meaning to. For example when people have heart surgery, hip surgery, and other major surgery or have illnesses, such as cancer, that transform their lives either for the good or bad, they often explore their inner spiritual selves and stretch into areas they have never gone before.

The Muslims' Hajj is a pilgrimage to Mecca, located in Saudi Arabia and its history dates back thousands of years back to the time of Ibrahim or Abraham. The Jews and Christians version of the pilgrimage is the story of Mary's and Joseph's pilgrimage to Jerusalem for the purpose of paying taxes (not so religious a purpose), when their son, Jesus, was born. What this story lacks in spiritual transformation is made up by Jesus' life, death, and resurrection.

The labyrinth was popular in the Middle Ages as a way to pilgrimage for repentance, which some scholars report was walked on one's knees. It was also used as a substitute for a pilgrimage to Jerusalem. This was so popular that some labyrinths were referred to as "the road to Jerusalem." The one remaining labyrinth from the Middle Ages was built in the 1200s and is located in the Chartres Cathedral near Paris, France. We now refer to the Chartres Labyrinth as an 11-rung labyrinth or the Cloverleaf Labyrinth.

Many pilgrimages don't depend on physically going on a journey as in the traveling sense, but they most definitely travel to a place far into the recesses of their mind. People who experience a serious life-threatening illness, such as cancer, or major surgery, such as open heart surgery, mastectomy, hip and other surgeries that restore mobility are often forced to look at themselves as if mirrors surrounded them on all sides reflecting all that they have or have not accomplished in their life. And as they recover, they often understand the pilgrimage that they have been on.

A single, retired woman that I know talked about a trip that she had taken. The trip had been planned as a pleasure trip, but all along the way she was faced with obstacles. Some of the obstacles were physical ones, such as not finding a hotel or motel when she thought she needed to rest. But other mental obstacles popped up in her path, such as the realization that she would have to eat a meal alone. As she reached the end of her journey and had safely returned home, she reflected on the things that had happened to her. She realized that she had been on a spiritual pilgrimage without knowing it. She resolved to make some changes in her life.

And so it happens as many of us as we travel our everyday, there are challenges that we must conquer. Planning a pilgrimage with the purpose of spiritual growth is not necessary; life seems to provide these stimulations when we need them.

A few years ago, however, my aunt took a pilgrimage to the Holy Lands. On the way, the group studied many Biblical passages that pertained to their location. When she returned, she told me that it had been an awesome experience. It had been so soulfully significant to her that she couldn't even explain it.

"There was just something about standing on the same ground or in the same building where Jesus had been," she said. "It was like stepping into a sacred time and space continuum."

Had she met Jesus on the road to Damascus? It is hard to say whether her experiences were that adventurous, but there was no discounting that her experience had been soul building.

When people encounter troubles in their lives and change because of it, they often feel as if they have been on a pilgrimage of sorts. When criminals go to prison and find God, they often have experienced the same soul-changing journey. The test is whether that experience truly transforms them and changes their behavior when they get out of prison.

When some people talk of angels guiding them, they, too, are experiencing a pilgrimage of sorts. So how can we recreate that same sort of pilgrimage? The labyrinth can often transport us into that sacred time and space continuum. Some people feel the shift into another place and time, while others do not.

At a women's conference in the hills of Arkansas, one of the women in attendance built a labyrinth. In the center was the shape of a Goddess. When I first saw the labyrinth in the dark, I just saw squiggly lines. But as I walked, I felt a strong presence. It was like saying a prayer in the presence of a Holy One or a Light Being (some people call them angels or spirits or energy beings). The closer I got to the center, the stronger it felt. Others were walking the labyrinth with me, but I did not see them. The experience was so powerful that it drew me to tears. I actually cried after returning to my room, but I could not explain why or what I felt. It was a very profound feeling that touched my soul and afterwards I was not the same person...I had experienced a transformation.

Pilgrimages on or off the labyrinth can be taken without leaving town or even the room that we are in. We simply begin on a journey that takes us into our soul. Of course, there are many tools that we might use to help us on our pilgrimage, especially pilgrimages on a labyrinth.

Meditation

Meditation is often used in conjunction with the labyrinth. To get the greatest benefit out of the experience, you can use it like a prayer or wish. You can put into your mind something that you need or something that you need to get rid of in your life. You can think of both. It is sort of shedding one thing and taking on another or going into that life-death-life process.

While solitude is often used for meditating, listening to certain music, such as classical, new age or Christian music often puts you in the mood of meditating. But sounds during meditation are not essential. And though there may actually be some distracting sounds, through focusing your mind on just the one prayer, wish, aspect to take on or get rid of, you can block out the world around you.

Walking the labyrinth is its own meditation. It should be done slowly and with thoughtfulness or prayerfully. Often, I have walked with the soul focus of listening to my own body rhythms. With every step, you can move to your own heart beat.

People who know how to meditate can often control stress. When stress levels begin to rise, it is possible to take deep breaths and with each exhale release the stress. Meditation takes you into yourself in many ways on many levels.

Buddhists meditate by concentrating on the breath alone. Your mind is not fixed upon any one idea, in fact, during a Buddhist meditation, the idea is to remove all thoughts and concentrate only on the breath. It is often described as watching a river, seeing your thoughts floating down the river. But you don't grab hold of the thoughts, instead you watch them float by and concentrate only on the breath.

Meditation can also be done through chanting. The Gregorian Monks are rather famous for their chanting. Tapes of their chanting can be purchased and used during meditation. Or, you can learn some chants for yourself. The idea is that you repeat a phrase over and over. Sometimes a chant can be more like a prayer than a chant and can be used as the object of your meditation.

For example, a healing chant for a particular person might be used. For the sake of illustration, let's name our recipient Donna. A healing chant might sound like: Donna, get well, or Donna, please heal. You repeat the words: *Donna, get well…Donna, get well…Donna, get well*, over and over during your meditation or while you are walking the labyrinth. Meditative chants should be simple, but you don't need anything special to create them.

A chant can also act as the focal point for meditation. Using a chant in this respect is almost the same as concentrating on your breath. You concentrate on the sound, instead. For example, repeat and draw out the sound of *ohm*. This is often used in yoga meditations. The sound helps us concentrate and lose ourselves in the sound, thoughts then are easily dismissed and meditation achieved.

Drumming is also used during meditation. Like chanting, the drumbeats are the focal point. Listening to drumming resembles keying into our own heartbeats. Drumming is also used in a particular form of meditation called journeying.

Guided meditations take you on a particular journey. At the end of this booklet, there is a guided meditation entitled "Wild Guided Meditation." This type of meditation is generally set up to help you vision a place and a set of events for a particular purpose. Guided meditations resemble journeying.

Journeying and Directed Dreaming

Journeying is most often seen as a technique of meditation. However, many do this through drumming. Like the guided meditation, you set out to a specific place with a set of events. The outcome is usually to discover something about your inner self. The most common journeying is to find a spirit guide or to ask your spirit guide a question.

During this type of a journey, you can picture yourself in a familiar, safe place. One way to get to into the journey is to find a tree and follow it down to its roots and picture yourself following it down further and further until you come to another place. In this place, you will see animals and people. Each time you encounter an animal or person, you can ask if they are your spirit guide. When you encounter your own spirit guide, they will confirm that they are indeed your spirit guide. Once you've found a spirit guide, you can look for your guide and ask the guide a question. You can also look for additional guides. We, generally, have many spirit guides who help us through our lives.

Very much like the guided meditations, journeys take you to special places where you meet wise people or wise entities of some sort. You may ask these wise ones a question. It is through the questions that your spirituality or soul grows.

This is much like dreaming. I refer to it more as directed dreaming, because you usually have a direction that you wish for your dream to take. Some people can do directed dreaming at any time. Others must set up a more artificial setting for directed dreaming with incense and music or drumming tapes.

Queuing on the end of the music for waking or coming out of directed dreaming or journeying can be done. Drumming tapes generally have a change in the beat that is intended to bring you back. However, some people take this directed dreaming or journey as a precursor to a regular night's sleep, which means that they just simply go into regular sleep. Other people have some sort of internal clock that will queue them at the end of a certain time period. Most journey or directed dreaming can take place in a 15- or 20-minute time frame.

Another solution, of course, is to set your alarm clock to wake you at the end of your allotted time. Dreamtime has no connection to real time. Journeys that seem like days can take place in a matter of a few real minutes.

Images in Journeying and Directed Dreaming

Images are important to journeying and directed dreaming. In fact, some people focus on the image of whom or what they want to communicate with in their journey. However, even those who aren't aware of images prior to journeying find that vivid images stay with them.

Journeying and directed dreaming can be linked to regular dream imagery. However, unlike normal dreams, journeying is self-induced. But the images are usually strong in both instances. While there are plenty of books on dream images, I mostly believe that you can decipher what they mean to you.

Dream images seem more mysterious, because they often are giving us messages. A few years ago, I attended a dream workshop given by Kathleen Sullivan, a well-known dream therapist in California. In the workshop, she described recurring dreams that were often scary and nightmarish. Her belief, as a psychologist and dream therapist, is that dreams recur for a purpose. Her own experience was that the dreams were telling her what she needed to do with her life. Kathleen Sullivan also believes that dreamers can easily decode most dreams. When people most need a dream therapist is when their dreams disturb them and they cannot find a logical answer for them.

One helpful tool in dream work is to make it a journey. By directing your dream, you can confront the image or entity that disturbs you and ask what it means. For example, Kathleen Sullivan used the image of an eagle getting caught in a spider web. Until she realized that she was the eagle and that the eagle had to release itself from the web, her dream kept coming back. However, had Kathleen directed her dream, she might have been able to ask the eagle a question.

Not everyone has success at journeying or directing his or her dreams. But almost everyone comes into contact with images. Often these images seem to pop up as mere coincidence in our lives. But if we stop to analyze them, we often find that the Universe, God or Goddess was trying to tell us something.

Messages from heaven, so to speak, can be found within the images that we encounter. I'm not saying that watching your television image is a message. But sometimes we will be drawn to an image. For example, a turtle, butterfly or mermaid image may pull our attention to it repeatedly. This sort of image in our lives may help us decode the message from the mysterious Source, One, God, Goddess, or Universe.

Mandalas

As young children, we understand the peace of sitting and coloring patterns — in coloring books or our own original patterns. Drawing and coloring a horse, is drawing a pattern. Patterns exist in all facets of our life.

Mandala is a Sanskrit word or from the Eastern or Indian culture. Jung found Mandalas existed within acute psychic chaos, possibly as a self-healing tendency of the soul. One of the more popular Mandala patterns are the Rose Windows of Gothic architecture. They sprang up during a time of chaos.

Over the years, those who have studied Mandalas have found these patterns exist in all cultures and may be the one connection that transcends all spiritual paths and have great healing qualities.

Looking at our brain, we see a remarkable resemblance to a Mandala and a labyrinth. Its two halves can be seen as polar, which is often found in the Mandala and represented in the T'ai Chi signs or Yin and Yang symbol. We also see the four segments of the circle representing the directions or four seasons as in Changing

A Spider, Some Thread, and a Labyrinth Walk

Woman, a Native American story about how the seasons came about.

When we understand that the Mandala represents existence in its most primal or spiritual level, we understand its representation of the God, Goddess, One, Source or Universe and the many other names we might use. The principle of the Mandala makes us aware of the *inside* and *outside* status of the world in which we exist. The Mandala is a circle and what is *inside* the circle can represent our *internal world, our thought world, our soul*, while the *outside* portion of the circle might be seen as the *physical world* we live in. Both exist simultaneously.

We can use the Mandala to draw our symbols for what we need now. We can use the Mandala as a meditation or focusing tool. Or we can combine the two together. The Mandala is a flexible tool with no right or wrong way to create them. The labyrinth is a Mandala for which we can physically get inside.

When we explore the patterns in our life, we find the Mandala is everywhere. Our earth is a Mandala, our oceans filled with water droplets — all are Mandalas. The rocks on the land, in the mountains, and what make up the soil are all structures of minerals, which are crystals. Crystals form Mandalas, cells are Mandalas, and atoms are Mandalas. At our basic core, Mandalas exists or should I say: at our core, we are Mandalas. Each of our Chakras (also a Sanskrit word that translates loosely to energy wheels) are also Mandalas.

Mandalas are also about movement, although we often see them as a static pattern on a stationary piece of paper. When using a Mandala as a focus tool, we find it resets our internal awareness. The Mandalas spin and spiral just as our *Chakras* spin. Our auras connect our bodies into a Mandala or Chakra and our DNA forms a Mandala spiral.

Inside we are moved by the Mandala pattern. Spiritually, we are moved by these patterns. When walking a labyrinth, we are walking the pattern of a Mandala. We follow the circular or spiral patterns toward the center; thus, we have created a Mandala in our movement. As we meditate, we circle around a center or focus point. Therefore, we create a Mandala.

The creation myths indicate a hidden Mandala. For example, "In the beginning was the Word." A word indicates sound and sound emanates from a point or center in spherical waves much like a stone making rings in the water. Some myths have the beginning as light, but again it radiates from a center. These centers are the center point of a circle or Mandala. As we begin to understand the Mandala as representing creation, we can see the Mandala as a means to communicate with that source.

Mandalas seem to incorporate a wide-range of connections, such as: labyrinth; pilgrimage; meditation; journeying, dreaming; prayer; art; sacred space; spiritual path; images and ritual. The Mandala can also be used as a form of journal. Many people keep journals of all sorts. The Mandala journal would be more of a meditative art journal.

To begin creating a Mandala, draw a circle. This makes a beautiful picture if you use black paper and a soft white pencil. You may also use an array of colors on this to create a simulation of stained glass.

The Mandala drawings are beautiful. Even if you don't consider yourself an artist, you can draw Mandalas. Once the circle is created, you can use any geometric design within it to create some interesting shapes and designs.

A Spider, Some Thread, and a Labyrinth Walk

ABOUT MAGIC

We live in a world full of magic and wonder. The everyday miracles that happen in our society seem so mundane in comparison to the glitz and glamour of television, movies and computerized games that many of us no longer even see the magic that is happening all around us.

Miraculous things seem to only happen in movies, because we look for things that are much too big. There are many miracles or magical happenings in this world that are tiny and everyday. For example, a baby being born no longer seems miraculous or wonderful or magical. It begins with a microscopic egg and sperm, yet, baby and all its parts come from a mysterious process that our bodies know instinctively how to perform. The DNA tells the cells to split and change and form every organ and every part of what becomes a human.

The process of a caterpillar turning into a butterfly is also magical. Imagine that plump little worm turning into a beautiful butterfly.

The leaves turning color in the fall and budding out in the spring are also miracles of life. But, too often, we become so busy that we aren't aware of these miraculous surroundings.

A few years ago, an Oprah Winfrey show was devoted to miracles. People talked about medical problems that miraculously disappeared after prayers were said. One man even died on an operating table and CPR was done for more than an hour in hopes of reviving him, when the medical professionals finally gave up on him, he revived on his own. At the exact same time that he revived, his wife was saying prayers.

Shamans and medicine men and women have been miraculous curing people for thousands of year. One medicine man explained that the cure came when he and his patient journeyed together into the underworld or shadow world and he could see what was wrong. Once he could see what was wrong, he could help his patient fix the problem. While the problem showed up as a medical problem, the cure happened when the spirit was set free.

The workings of life are more magic that our society will allow us to see. Even many Christian teachings will not allow for the depth of magic that exists. The power of prayer or good thoughts by a group can be very awesome.

As a healer, I know there are people who are beyond skeptic. I, myself, have been there in the past, and I also know that some illnesses cannot be cured. When you cannot heal an illness, you can, at least, give them some peace, help them with anxiety. But healing isn't really magic. While there isn't any direct scientific explanation, we know that everything and everyone are simply energy. And healing is simply opening up the energy flow in your body or sending them energy where they need it.

Not everyone feels or sees energy; however, that does not mean that it doesn't exist. You see, there are chakras or energy wheels that are located down our spine; starting at the bottom and going up there are seven.

Meanings of Magic

To many people, *magic* means something gaudy, cheap, showy or vulgar. It has been linked to *Magic Shows*, which use the art of illusion to deceive an audience into believing one thing happened when something else actually took place. For example, *sawing a woman in half* appears real enough, but it is actually a work of trickery. This is not *real magic*.

Other people associate magic with the special effects created by film and television artists. This is so totally NOT magic! Although the words *magic maker* has often been used to describe directors and producers, we must understand that this, too, is an illusion. It is an art form. The razzle and dazzle that transport us to a different time and place with all the sights and sounds to match the imaginary world of film and television is not *real magic*.

Magic products that clean away something in an instant, transform the smells in a room or otherwise make cleaning a supposedly magical experience are all illusions. Most of the time the advertising surrounding products is mostly illusion to make you believe that this product is better than its competitors! Often, the product does not measure up.

Real Magic and Where You Find It

Finding *MAGIC* in the spiritual sense means that we must go inside ourselves and find the miraculous things that both make us human and that transcend us from being human.

For example: Have you ever walked into a room and felt the energy of the room? When other people are in the room, their energies are combined and give off a distinct energy. Some people feel it and call it by other names. For example, if you've ever walked into a meeting where problems were being discussed, you know what energy feels like. It is hard to miss. It's like reading the temperature. You know when people are upset before they ever speak. This is *magic*.

Real magic is hard to explain, because it is connected to what we often refer to as the *supernatural*. The term *supernatural* falls into the illusions of many things, such as the existence of alien beings. But some *supernatural* is simply *magic*. It is often difficult for us to tell the *real magic* from illusion, and, in some cases, maybe arguing the difference is unnecessary.

You know it is *magic* when you suddenly understand an animal. I heard a woman talk about communicating with animals. They don't use words like we do, but you can communicate with them by understanding the magical use of telepathy. Telepathy has been dismissed as an art of illusion in the past. However, telepathy is more real than some are ready to acknowledge. It is the language of our Mother Earth, the Goddess Earth, speaking to us through the beauty of the plants and trees. And maybe it isn't real *telepath*, but should have a different name. Whatever we want to call it, this is *magic*! Sometimes we see communications with another being as graphic images and sometimes we see the actual words. Most often we hear people referring to this as *otherworld* knowing or *intuition*. I think when *real magic* has appeared in your life, you know it to be authentic.

Magic refers to more than simply communications, but communicating is the key to almost everything. When you witness a beautiful sunset and you are reminded that life has its beautiful moments: *That's Magic!* When Goddesses and Gods begin to communicate with you, then you know *magic*! Although these are mostly mythical beings, they do work as archetypes in our lives. I know they speak to us through dreams, because my goddess, Yemaya (Yim-mah-yah) gives me messages that often come through dreams. She also causes me to be somewhat distracted at times and miss turns, because I need to see something where I go or something bad might have happened to me where I was.

When unexplained things happen to us that we might otherwise see as our own mistakes, magic may have happened. You may have gotten sidetracked by a god or goddess…or maybe God or the Mystery that some people call God or the Universe.

Magic can also be spontaneous acts of generosity.

The Magic of Imagination and Storytelling

For those who are still a bit skeptic about magic, this discussion might help. Who can deny that there is magic in imagination? If you've ever watched a child, you'd know magic was alive and well. The imagination of children is absolutely magical, indeed.

When storytelling, you know you've reached that magical place when everyone gets quiet. They are quiet, because you've got the audience spellbound. It's where I like my audiences to stay. On the other end, being on the recipient end of storytelling, you know there is magic when the story takes you to a magical place. That magical place doesn't have to be a physical magical place. Sometimes it's when the story has touched you deeply.

A long time ago, I had a friend who said that the test of whether a movie was magic is when it makes you cry. I don't think you have to necessarily cry, but what happens when you do cry is that you've been moved emotionally.

ABOUT THE AUTHOR

Connie Dunn is an author. She is also a writing, publishing, and creativity coach, who coaches writers from idea through published book. Self-publishing is Connie's specialty.

She is an educator with a long history of working as a religious educator for Unitarian Universalist churches. She also teaches creativity workshops, such as making magic wands and plaster masks. When artists, musicians, and writers hit a time when they cannot create, she helps them get over their obstacle.

Connie has a bachelor's degree in Marketing and Small Business Management. She has been writing all her life and spent more than 20 years as a freelance writer and had a regular column in such publications as The Dallas Morning News. This column earned her an award from the SBA for her work with Home-Based Businesses.

Connie is also a Certified Master Life Coach, Certified Master Neuro Linguistic Programming (NLP) Practitioner and Trainer, Master Reiki Practitioner, Vibrational Therapist (includes Color, Sound, Crystals, and Aroma Therapies), and Credentialed Religious Educator. She uses all her training to help people find their authentic self and their creative voice.

Connie's newest books:

The Most Magical, Awesome, Delicate Creature of All (a new myth about how butterflies came to be)
Website: http://magicalawesomedelicatecreature.webs.com

Trees: Peaceful and Personal Meditational Poems
Website: http://www.trees-meditate.com

Goddess Rituals: Reclaiming Our Ancient Spiritual Heritage
Website: http://goddessrituals.webs.com

Miss Odell: the Privileges of Being Present for the End of Her Life – A Reality Book on Caring for an Elder
Website: http://www.missodell-realitybook.com

www.ingramcontent.com/pod-product-compliance
Lightning Source LLC
Chambersburg PA
CBHW031211090426
42736CB00009B/869